PEOPLE AT THE CENTER OF

THE FRENCH REVOLUTION

By GAIL B. STEWART

BLACKBIRCH PRESS
An imprint of Thomson Gale, a part of The Thomson Corporation

THOMSON
GALE

Detroit • New York • San Francisco • San Diego • New Haven, Conn. • Waterville, Maine • London • Munich

THOMSON

GALE

™

Picture Credits: Cover: Napoleon: Giraudon/Art Resource, N.Y.; Robespierre: Archivo Iconografico,S.A.; Main: Reunion des Musees Nationaux/Art Resource, N.Y.; The Art Archive/Chateau de Blois/Dagli Orti, 38; The Art Archive/Marc Charmet, 14, 24; The Art Archive/Musee Carnavalet Paris/Dagli Orti, 15; The Art Archive/Musee des Beaux Arts Nantes/Dagli Orti, 39; Giraudon/Art Resource, N.Y., 9, 18; Erich Lessing/Art Resource,N.Y., 19, 32, 37, 45; The New York Public Library/Art Resource,N.Y., 13; Reunion des Musee Nationaux/Art Resource,N.Y., 11, 17, 34, 43, 44; Snark/Art Resource, N.Y. 36; © Archivo Iconografico,S.A., 5, 26, 35, 40; © Bettmann/CORBIS, 12; © Ali Meyer/CORBIS, 16; © Gianni Dagli Orti/CORBIS, 32, 41; © Leonard de Silva/CORBIS, 33; Hulton Archive by Getty Images, 20, 22–23; Time-Life Pictures/Getty Images, 10; Mary Evans Picture Library, 8; Mary Evans Picture Library/Fae Fallon, 27–28; North Wind Picture Archives, 7, 25

LIBRARY OF CONGRESS CATALOGING-IN-PUBLICATION DATA

Stewart, Gail B., 1949–
  The French Revolution / by Gail B. Stewart.
    p. cm. — (People at the center of)
  Includes bibliographical references and index.
  ISBN 1-56711-919-0 (hard cover : alk. paper)
  1. France—History—Revolution, 1789–1799. I. Title. II. Series.
  DC148.S84 2005
  944.04—dc22

2005001875

Printed in the United States of America

CONTENTS

PEOPLE AT THE CENTER OF

THE FRENCH REVOLUTION

The French Revolution forever changed the way France was governed and how its society was organized. The Revolution took place in the late eighteenth century, spanning ten years of the most violent, unsettling times in that nation's history. It was not a war, as was the American Revolution, that was fought because people wanted their independence from a colonial power. Instead, it was a period of political upheaval during which the French people rebelled against their old system of government, which seemed to them outdated and unfair.

Although the Revolution officially began in 1789, the events that set it in motion began long before that date. During the period called the Enlightenment, which took place during the seventeenth and eighteenth centuries in France and elsewhere, new thinking challenged the old ways of looking at religion and politics. Jean-Jacques Rousseau, for example, wrote in his famous work *The Social Contract* that governments were useless unless they reflected the will of the people. Other writers agreed, challenging the idea of the divine right of kings, which held that a monarch's power was given to him by God.

The concepts that people could make their own laws and have a voice in their government were exciting new ideas in eighteenth-century France. France, like other European nations, had a monarchy in which the king held absolute power. There was also a strict social order. The three segments of French society were called estates. Members of the First Estate were the clergy, and the wealthy nobility comprised the Second Estate. The largest group was the Third Estate, made up of the poorest citizens and common people. But although they were the largest group, they had the least power. Though some made barely enough money to feed their families, they bore a heavier tax burden than those in the First or Second estates.

It was a financial crisis that set off the Revolution. Many years of heavy military expenses, in addition to lavish spending by the throne, had left the royal treasury almost empty. The poorest citizens of France usually paid the most taxes, but scant harvests had all but ruined many farmers. Bread was scarce, and many people were on the verge of starvation. To show their displeasure and frustration, thousands of poor people rioted throughout the country. Hoping to find ways to raise money and

On July 14, 1789, French citizens storm the Bastille, an enormous prison in the heart of Paris. The event marked the beginning of the French Revolution.

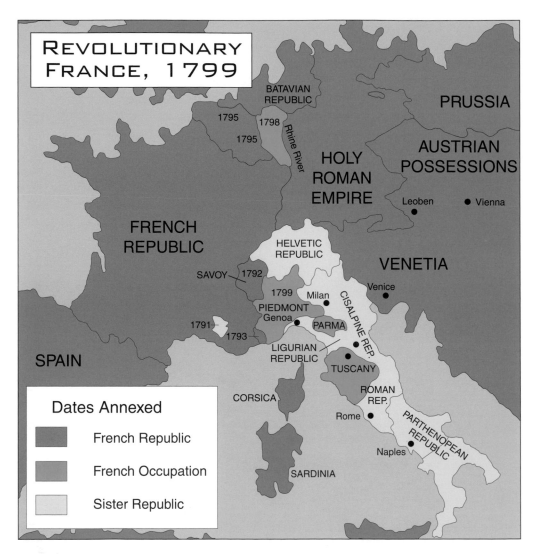

REVOLUTIONARY FRANCE, 1799

BATAVIAN REPUBLIC

PRUSSIA

1795

1798

1795

Rhine River

HOLY ROMAN EMPIRE

AUSTRIAN POSSESSIONS

Leoben

Vienna

FRENCH REPUBLIC

HELVETIC REPUBLIC

SAVOY

1792

VENETIA

1799

Milan

Venice

PIEDMONT

CISALPINE REP.

Genoa

1791

PARMA

1793

LIGURIAN REPUBLIC

SPAIN

TUSCANY

CORSICA

ROMAN REP.

Rome

PARTHENOPEAN REPUBLIC

Naples

SARDINIA

Dates Annexed

French Republic

French Occupation

Sister Republic

calm the unrest, the king called an assembly known as the Estates-General, a group comprising representatives from each of the three estates. They began their meetings on May 5, 1789.

The representatives of the Third Estate hoped that the king would at least consider reforms that would help the common people, but it soon became apparent that Louis XVI had no intention of doing so. Instead, the privileged estates repeatedly blocked whatever reforms the Third Estate proposed. Finally, on June 17, 1789, the leaders of the Third Estate walked out of the assembly, vowing to form the National Assembly, which would be the one true representative body in France. They welcomed any representatives from the other estates who wished to join them, but insisted that they would have no more privileges than any other representatives.

Louis XVI outwardly accepted the National Assembly. Behind the scenes, however, he tried to undermine its efforts. He ordered his troops to lock the doors of the assembly hall so the new group could not meet. In response, the members of the National Assembly moved to an indoor tennis court nearby and made a solemn vow that they would not disperse until they had written a new constitution for France. The king and his outraged nobles agreed to recognize the National Assembly as official, for there were not enough troops in Paris to fight the large number of assembly delegates.

The courageous move by the National Assembly was the beginning of the French Revolution. At the time the Tennis Court Oath was taken, many representatives of the National Assembly believed that France could change its form of government to a constitutional monarchy, in which the king would rule, but his powers would be

Members of the Third Estate walk out in anger from the Estates-General, frustrated that none of their reforms had passed.

limited by an active legislative assembly. If Louis and the privileged estates had agreed to it, the Revolution might have ended there. But they did not.

Instead, the king worked against the reforms, even plotting with foreign leaders to upset the new government so he could regain his power. Louis was jailed as a traitor, and in 1793 he was beheaded by the sharp blade of the guillotine. From then on, the nation skidded into the most violent time in its history. Revolutionary leaders disagreed on how the new government should be run, and by whom. The Girondists, moderate leaders who favored a constitutional monarchy, were driven out of power by more radical leaders called the Jacobins, who accused them of treason. The Jacobin leaders, who were in favor of setting up a democratic republic, formed a citizens' army to fight the Girondist rebels. During this time, known as the Reign of Terror, more than two hundred thousand people suspected of being enemies of the state were jailed, and more than eighteen thousand were executed.

In 1793 the severed head of King Louis XVI is displayed to a mob of onlookers in Paris.

Victims of the Reign of Terror are loaded onto carts for a mass burial outside the city walls of Paris.

At the same time, Austria, Prussia, and other European nations tried to keep revolutionary activity from spreading across their borders by attacking France. In 1799 the French Revolution ended when the powerful French general Napoleon Bonaparte and his supporters took over the floundering government and created a new constitution.

The Revolution did not result in the free, democratic society that many of its original leaders had hoped for. It did transform France, however. No longer did the country have a social and political system based on inherited wealth. No longer were the poorest citizens required to pay the highest taxes and suffer as they had under the old system. The ancient regime had ended, and the French people finally had a voice in their government—an enormous accomplishment.

JEAN-JACQUES ROUSSEAU

ADVOCATE OF SOCIAL JUSTICE

Jean-Jacques Rousseau was born on June 28, 1712, in Geneva, Switzerland. When he was fifteen, he left his home and traveled though Europe, working at a series of jobs. He moved to Paris in 1741.

Paris was at the height of the Enlightenment when Rousseau arrived. Exciting new ideas about liberty, social justice, and religion were being discussed, as were new advances in science and art. Throughout the city there were lectures and intellectual conversations about these subjects, and Rousseau attended as many as he could. In 1749 he entered an essay contest on the topic of morality and science, and when he won, he became an instant celebrity.

Rousseau wrote a number of books and essays on social and political ideas. His most important work dealt with humanity's need for equality and freedom.

Opposite: Jean-Jacques Rousseau was a champion of democracy during the Enlightenment. Above: An angry mob burns copies of Rousseau's Social Contract.

Like many Enlightenment thinkers, Rousseau believed that governments such as France's monarchy had abused their power. He felt that this type of government had led to inequality and an imbalance among its citizens. While the wealthy had power and owned a great deal of property, the vast majority of citizens had neither.

In 1762 Rousseau wrote his most well-known work, called *The Social Contract*. In it he explained that governments should be sensitive to the needs of all people. He believed that the only government that could do this was a democracy, in which all citizens had a voice in making laws. The right to govern did not come from God, he argued, but from the citizens of the country. This was very controversial, for at that time, monarchs such as Louis XVI believed that their right to govern was ordained by God.

Rousseau was a gifted writer, and his ideas became popular with his readers. Although he died in 1778—eleven years before the French Revolution began—his important ideas about freedom and government influenced many of the revolution's leaders.

THOMAS PAINE

Thomas Paine was born on January 29, 1737, in Norfolk County, England. He was not interested in becoming a tradesman like his father, preferring instead to think about politics and philosophy. As a young man, he wrote essays on topics he found fascinating, such as taxation, poverty, and the purpose of government.

While in London, Paine met Benjamin Franklin. The American diplomat was attempting to work out a peaceful solution to the hostility growing between the American colonies and King George III of England, who wanted to increase the colonists' taxes. Franklin was impressed with Paine, and urged him to visit America. Paine sailed to America in 1774, and began writing essays about the importance of independence for the American colonies.

Paine's most important work, called *Common Sense*, was published in 1776. It was a forty-two page booklet that criticized George III and praised the American colonists for seeking liberty. His book became the first American bestseller—more than 120,000 copies were sold in twelve weeks. *Common Sense* was inspirational in rousing Americans to fight for their freedom.

Americans were not the only ones who appreciated Paine's work, however. His essays about liberty were an important motivating factor in the early days of the French Revolution. Knowing that revolution was possible, and that Paine's work had inspired the Americans to victory, made a great impression on French revolutionary leaders and common people alike.

Paine visited France after the American Revolution, and in 1792 he became a French citizen. He later became a member of the National Convention, the legislative body that was created after the removal of King Louis XVI. Paine was a Girondist, a member of the more moderate of the parties in the convention. When the more extreme Jacobins accused the Girondists of treason and forced them from the convention, Paine and other Girondists were imprisoned.

Paine remained in prison for almost a year, until James Monroe, the American ambassador to France, secured his release. In 1802 Paine returned to the United States, where he died in 1809.

COMMON SENSE;

ADDRESSED TO THE

INHABITANTS

OF

AMERICA,

On the following interesting

SUBJECTS.

I. Of the Origin and Design of Government in general, with concise Remarks on the English Conftitution.

II. Of Monarchy and Hereditary Succeſſion.

III. Thoughts on the preſent State of American Affairs.

IV. Of the preſent Ability of America, with ſome miſcellaneous Reflections.

A NEW EDITION, with ſeveral Additions in the Body of the Work. To which is added an APPENDIX; together with an Addreſs to the People called QUAKERS.

N. B. The New Addition here given increaſes the Work upwards of One-Third.

Man knows no Maſter ſave creating Heaven, Or thoſe whom Choice and Common Good ordain.

THOMSON.

PHILADELPHIA, PRINTED;

Opposite: Thomas Paine urged the American colonies to revolt against Great Britain. Above: Published in 1776, Paine's Common Sense *was the first work to champion American independence.*

Louis-Auguste was born at the French royal palace of Versailles on August 23, 1754. He was the grandson of King Louis XV. When the boy's father and two older brothers died, he became the next in line to the throne of France. In 1770, at the age of sixteen, Louis married the beautiful Marie Antoinette of Austria in an arranged marriage intended to ensure good relations between the two nations. In 1774 Louis XV died, and Louis XVI became king at the age of twenty.

Opposite: King Louis XVI was the ineffectual ruler of France at the time of the French Revolution. Above: King Louis addresses an angry mob from the balcony of Versailles.

Though he was smart and kindhearted, Louis was a weak king. He was shy and preferred to take long walks in the woods near the palace rather than mingle with the privileged aristocrats who were a constant presence at the court. He also disliked having to tell others what to do.

France, however, needed a strong, capable leader. The nation was in debt from a series of wars that had emptied its treasury—including the expense of helping the Americans fight the British in the Revolutionary War. The lower classes, known as the Third Estate, resented being asked to give more in taxes to make up the shortfall when wealthier people were not even expected to pay taxes. They demanded that Louis create reforms to help them. But Louis was unwilling to limit the privileges of the wealthiest subjects or force them to pay taxes. As France's finances worsened, the anger of the Third Estate increased.

By the summer of 1789, Louis had lost the support of many of the Third Estate, who realized their king would not come to their aid. There was rioting throughout the country, and in October an angry mob forced Louis and his family from their palace in Versailles. The mob demanded that the royal family be held as prisoners in Paris.

Virtually stripped of his powers, Louis tried to flee from France. He hoped to get help from foreign armies to stop the growing revolution. He was captured, however, and was later tried for treason. He was executed on January 21, 1793. Because of his arrest and execution, Louis became one of the most important figures of the Revolution. By killing their king, the French revolutionaries demonstrated to the world that they would no longer be ruled by a monarch, but instead would be governed by the will of the people.

Marie-Antoinette

Marie-Antoinette was born in Vienna, Austria, on November 2, 1755. Her parents were Empress Maria Theresa and Francis I, the rulers of Austria. As was common at the time, her marriage to Louis XVI was arranged when she was very young. The couple wed in 1770, and Louis ascended to the throne four years later. Marie-Antoinette became queen of France at age nineteen.

The new queen was very different from her husband. She enjoyed parties and social events. She spent a great deal of money on decorating, entertaining, and gambling. She also gave gifts of money to her friends. At this time France was in financial trouble; overspending on wars had all but emptied the national treasury. And though Louis and his ministers warned her about the financial crisis, she paid little attention and continued her lavish spending.

When the Revolution began in 1789, she urged Louis to remain firm and to refuse to compromise with leaders of the National Assembly. Her mother had taught her that rulers were absolute, meaning that it was wrong to allow any legislative assembly to help make laws for the nation. She insisted that Louis not even consider a compromise to create a constitutional monarchy or other reforms in France.

As the Revolution continued, Marie-Antoinette became more and more hated by the common people, whose taxes were paying for her extravagant

Opposite: Foreign-born Marie-Antoinette was the hated wife of King Louis XVI. Above: Revolutionaries lead Marie to her execution in 1793.

lifestyle. A widely circulated story at the time was intended to illustrate how insensitive she was to the people's financial troubles. She supposedly asked why the poor were angry, and, when told that they had no bread, replied haughtily, "Then let them eat cake." Though not true, this story helped make the queen a symbol of the wealthy who opposed reforms that might help the common people.

On June 20, 1791, Marie-Antoinette convinced Louis that they should secretly flee to Austria. Once there, they could assemble an army friendly to the French throne and stamp out the Revolution once and for all. They were caught, however, and afterward were virtual prisoners. Marie-Antoinette was executed as a traitor ten months after Louis, on October 16, 1793.

JACQUES NECKER

FRENCH FINANCE MINISTER

Jacques Necker was born in Geneva, Switzerland, on September 30, 1732. He was an excellent student, finishing his secondary education at age fourteen—nearly four years ahead of his peers. He went to work as a banker's assistant and soon was tranferred to Paris.

There, he was appointed finance minister by Louis XVI in 1777. Necker was a talented financier, but he knew the job would be extremely difficult, for France faced dire economic problems. Overspending by the government had increased the nation's debt. When the French government agreed to help the American colonists fight the British in the Revolutionary War, the debt grew even larger.

Necker did not want to raise taxes for the common people, because he understood that they were already carrying too large a portion of the nation's burden. The nobility were critical of Necker, for they wanted taxes raised, knowing that they would pay very little themselves. In 1781 he angered them even more by publishing his famous *State of the Finances of France*, which clearly demonstrated how taxes were spent. It showed how much of the nation's wealth was spent by the royalty and their friends. It was important because it was the first time documented evidence was presented of the waste of the government and its favoritism toward the rich.

Opposite: As finance minister under Louis XVI, Jacques Necker tried unsuccessfully to solve France's dire economic problems. Above: Revolutionaries protest Necker's dismissal in 1789.

To save Louis XVI the trouble of firing him, Necker resigned that same year. He was brought back in 1788, however, because new finance ministers were unable to find a solution to the crisis. Necker believed that the tax burden must be shared, but the king lacked the strength and decisiveness to put Necker's ideas into motion. Louis was too intimidated by the aristocrats and nobles to demand reforms. Therefore, instead of being a voice for change, Necker became a scapegoat for the nation's financial problems.

Necker finally resigned for good in 1790, and spent the rest of his life reading and writing. He completed a three-volume history of the French Revolution in 1796. He died in Coppet, Switzerland, on April 9, 1804.

Emmanuel Sieyes was born in Frejus, France, on May 3, 1748. He later studied to be a priest, but found that he enjoyed reading the philosophical writings of Enlightenment thinkers such as Rousseau and John Locke as much as he enjoyed religious ones. Nevertheless, he entered the priesthood and became a church leader in the city of Chartres.

When King Louis XVI called for the Estates-General to assemble in 1789, Sieyes wrote a pamphlet entitled *What Is the Third Estate?* In it he tried to explain the importance of the common people, and how they had been ignored throughout France's history. He argued that the Third Estate was like a strong man who had one arm in chains. His pamphlet, one of hundreds that circulated at this time, was one of the most widely discussed. Members of the Third Estate considered him a champion of their rights, and revolutionary leaders frequently used his comparison of the man in chains in their speeches.

Although Sieyes, as a clergyman, belonged to the privileged First Estate, he eagerly agreed to represent the Third Estate in the Estates-General. When it became clear after a few days that Louis had no intention of reforming the voting process of the assembly (each estate got one vote, regardless of the number of delegates) the representatives of the Third Estate were angry. It was Sieyes who suggested that the frustrated delegates declare themselves the official National Assembly of France. If they stood in unison on this issue, he urged, they would be heard.

When the king's troops locked the assembly door so the new group could not meet, they assembled in a nearby indoor tennis court. Sieyes helped write an announcement known as the Tennis Court Oath. In the oath, the delegates swore that they would stand united until they were allowed to draft a new constitution that diminished the king's power and increased that of the legislature. Louis realized his troops were greatly outnumbered, and allowed the delegates to meet.

Although as a clergyman Emmanuel Sieyes belonged to the privileged First Estate, he represented the interests of the Third Estate during the Estates-General.

Sieyes served as president of the National Assembly in 1790, but because he was a poor public speaker, he did not rise in the leadership of the Revolution. He served as ambassador to Berlin in 1798, and then left public life. He died in 1836.

On June 20, 1789, members of the Third Estate swear to uphold the provisions of the Tennis Court Oath.

BERNARD DE LAUNAY

GUARDIAN OF THE BASTILLE

Bernard de Launay was born in Paris in 1740. His father had been the governor of a fortress called the Bastille. When de Launay grew up, he took over the position. Not only did he manage the daily affairs of the Bastille, but he lived within its walls.

The Bastille had become a hated symbol of injustice in France. For hundreds of years, people arrested by order of the king had been held there. Its nine-foot-thick walls made it an ideal prison, and those unfortunate enough to be sent there were tortured and beaten daily. Though it was not used as often as a prison by the time Louis XVI was king, it remained a storage area for ammunition and weapons for France's army.

De Launay was at the Bastille on July 14, 1789, when a large mob stormed its gates. They had heard rumors that Louis had called the army to disband the National Assembly. Refusing to be bullied by the king's army, the people decided to arm themselves. After obtaining some weapons at an armory, they arrived at the Bastille, hoping to seize the gunpowder and ammunition locked inside.

Opposite: Bernard de Launay, the governor of the Bastille, is killed as revolutionaries storm the prison. Above: A mob marches through Paris with de Launay's head on a pike.

De Launay refused to let the people in, and ordered them to leave. A few guards inside the Bastille fired on the crowd, which accomplished nothing. Realizing that the gates of the fortress could not hold out long against the mob, de Launay asked for a truce. The mob refused, and pushed open the gates. They captured de Launay and beat him to death. His head was put on a pike and paraded through the streets of Paris.

De Launay's death was tremendously important for a number of reasons. It showed Louis—as well as the other monarchs in Europe—what they had to fear from the common people who considered themselves victims of unfair government. Many of Europe's royalty were appalled, too, at the idea that a governor could be killed after offering a truce. The death of de Launay, more than any other event, made other European leaders fearful of the French Revolution, and willing to send troops to help Louis keep his throne.

Lafayette, whose real name was Gilbert du Montier, was born in Haute-Loire, France, on September 6, 1757. He was descended from nobility, and chose to become a soldier as his father had been. This was a fairly peaceful time in French history, however, and young Lafayette had few opportunities to prove himself in battle.

In 1777 he decided to go to America to help General George Washington and his Continental Army fight the British. He was only nineteen at the time, but did well. Within a few months, he was given command of a division and fought in several key battles.

When he returned to France in 1782, he became fascinated with the growing talk of reform among many French people. Because Lafayette was from the noble class, his was an important voice supporting reform. He believed, as did many other moderates at the beginning of the Revolution, that there could be a constitutional monarchy in France, in which the king would have limited power ruling alongside an elected national assembly.

His views, however, made him unpopular with many of his peers among the nobility. As the Revolution gained momentum, the common people, too, distrusted Lafayette because of his position in the National Guard, the king's army. By the summer of 1792, it was clear that he had lost the good name and reputation he once had. He tried without success to keep the Jacobins, the extremists in the Revolution, from disbanding the monarchy. The king and queen refused his assistance. Marie-Antoinette, the queen, even remarked that she would rather perish than be saved by such a man as Lafayette. He found, too, that when he ordered his National Guard to turn back a violent mob in Paris, the men would not follow his orders. Many of them even joined the mob. Fearing for his life, he fled the country, but was imprisoned by the Austrian army, which was at war with France. He remained in prison until 1797.

Although a nobleman by birth, the Marquis de Lafayette supported reform and believed France should be governed by a constitutional monarchy.

He returned to France in 1799, when the Revolution was over, and found that his fortune had been seized in his absence. Napoleon, a French general, took control of the government, and Lafayette agreed to serve France's new government as a respresentative to the Chamber of Deputies, the new legislative assembly in France. He died on May 20, 1834, in Paris.

The British surrender to George Washington, Lafayette, and other officers (on the left) at Yorktown, Virginia, in 1781.

COMTE MIRABEAU

THE "TRIBUNE OF THE PEOPLE"

Comte Mirabeau was born Honore Gabriel Riquetti in Bignon, France, on March 9, 1749. He entered a military school in Paris in 1767, and later became a cavalry officer. He had difficulty following and obeying orders, however, and was imprisoned more than once for misconduct.

Dissatisfied with military life, Mirabeau began to devote his time to reading and writing essays. He was interested in the revolutionary talk in France during the 1780s,

and found that although he was part of the noble class, he identified with the plight of the common people. When the members of the Third Estate rejected the Estates-General in May 1789, they formed their own National Assembly, inviting delegates from the First or Second Estate to join them. Mirabeau accepted quickly, and became a vocal member.

He soon became a legendary spokesman for the Third Estate. When the delegates for the common people formed their own legislative body, one of the king's ministers ordered them to disperse on June 23, 1789. Mirabeau

Opposite: Comte Mirabeau hoped to give the common people an expanded role in government. Above: Mirabeau defiantly tells a royal representative that the Third Estate will not disband.

responded in a loud voice that only by the point of a bayonet would they move from their assembly. After that incident, he became known as the "Tribune of the People."

Mirabeau wanted to work with the king to avoid violence. He hoped there could be reforms that could give the common people a role in government while allowing Louis to continue as a limited monarch. The royal family did not trust Mirabeau, however, and refused to initiate any reforms at all.

In 1790 Mirabeau joined the Jacobins, a radical group that favored the creation of a republic in France. Poor health forced him to resign from public life just a few months later, and he died on April 2, 1791. His three-mile-long funeral procession was one of the most spectacular in French history, joined by the entire National Assembly, the ministry, the army, and crowds of supporters from the common people.

JOSEPH-IGNACE GUILLOTIN

INVENTOR OF THE GUILLOTINE

Joseph-Ignace Guillotin was born on May 28, 1738, in Saintes, a city in western France. He did exceptionally well in school and decided to become a doctor. He graduated from the University of Paris in 1770.

In 1789 he was a delegate from the Third Estate of Paris to the National Assembly. Guillotin knew there were many other topics to be discussed at the assembly, but he was determined to propose reforms in the way death sentences were carried out. At the time, condemned prisoners were executed in a number of ways—slow hanging, burning, or, more commonly, quartering. To quarter a person meant to tie each of his or her limbs to one of four oxen, and then drive each beast in a different direction.

In December 1789 Guillotin argued that it would be far more humane to simply behead a condemned prisoner. He suggested using a machine that could do the job more quickly and more accurately than a swordsman could. His machine was a large, weighted blade that could be raised and dropped between two posts connected at the top by a crossbar. When allowed to drop, the blade fell with enough force to sever the head of a person lying below. A basket was placed in front, to catch the head.

Guillotin's proposal was passed by decree on March 25, 1791. Though Guillotin had no way of knowing it at the time, the machine (named the guillotine, after the man who had suggested its use) would become one of the most dreaded symbols of the French Revolution. In one year—between May 1793 and May 1794—more than one thousand people lost their heads to the guillotine in Paris alone. By 1799 more than fifteen thousand had been killed by what many called "the national razor."

Opposite: Joseph-Ignace Guillotin suggested the guillotine in 1789 as a humane method of execution. Above: King Louis XVI is led to the guillotine in 1793.

After Guillotin died in 1814, his children attempted to have the name of the machine changed. When they were unsuccessful, they changed their own last name instead.

GEORGES DANTON

Georges Danton was born in 1759, in Arcis-sur-Aube, France. He was a good student, and was not afraid to stand up for his friends. When he was sixteen, he objected when a teacher was going to beat a fellow student with a ruler. The principal of the school thought Danton's argument against such punishment so interesting that he refused to allow the beating.

When Louis XVI called the Estates-General in 1789, Danton was working in Paris as a lawyer. He was intrigued by the political activity associated with the Revolution, and decided to join the Jacobins, one of the political parties calling for radical change. Danton's strength was his speaking ability—he was a motivating and energetic orator, and could communicate the ideas of the Jacobins in a way that inspired his listeners.

Opposite: George Danton was one of the most radical members of the Jacobin political party. Above: Victims of the Jacobin Reign of Terror await execution.

In 1792 Danton became a leading delegate of the new assembly, the National Convention, that was formed after Louis XVI was removed from the throne. Danton urged that the king be executed for his refusal to help reform the government. Louis XVI was a traitor, Danton said, and must pay the price of treason.

Along with other noted Jacobins, including Jean-Paul Marat and Maximilien Robespierre, Danton helped force out the moderate members of the convention. He participated in the the most violent part of the Revolution, the Reign of Terror. During this time, thousands of people suspected of treason—or even suspected of disagreeing with the Revolution's leader—were executed.

In April 1793 the National Convention made Danton one of its nine-man Committee of Public Safety. This was a temporary government set up to rule France until the terms of a republic could be worked out. During this time, Danton became less supportive of the violence and called for an end to the executions. This angered Robespierre and the other radical Jacobins, and Danton himself was arrested as an enemy of the Revolution.

He was put on trial on March 29, 1794. Although he spoke brilliantly about the dangers of violence and the negative effects it would have on the Revolution, he was convicted and was executed on April 5, 1794.

JEAN-PAUL MARAT

INFLUENTIAL NEWSPAPER PUBLISHER

Jean-Paul Marat was born in Boudry, Switzerland, on May 24, 1743. Although his family was poor, his father was able to send him to medical school. He moved to Paris and became a successful doctor with practices in both France and England.

While medicine was his career, Marat's hobby was reading. He enjoyed learning about philosophy and politics, and was especially interested in the inequalities of the French social system. He was infuriated that the king and other royalty had all of the power, while the majority of the population was poor and powerless.

When the French Revolution began in 1789, Marat abandoned his medical practice and devoted his time to writing. In his newspaper, called *L'Ami du peuple* or *The People's Friend*, he urged the lower classes not to be satisfied with simply removing the king from power. Instead, he said, the Revolution would not be complete until everyone who opposed it was killed. Through his newspaper, Marat became one of the most important voices of the Revolution in Paris, pushing the poor to commit more and more violence.

In September 1792 there was a series of public executions known as the September Massacre. During this time of increased violence, Marat was elected to the newly formed legislative body called the National Convention, which replaced the monarchy. He was a key member of the extreme Jacobin party, which opposed the more moderate Girondist party.

Marat continued to publish his newspaper, and urged the overthrow of the Girondist leaders, whom he called enemies of the state. Marat's influence over the lower

Opposite: An influential newspaper publisher, Jean-Paul Marat wrote incendiary articles urging the people to violence. Above: Marat lies dead after being stabbed by Charlotte Corday.

classes was very strong; partly as a result of his editiorials, mobs threatened more violence unless the Girondists were expelled from the convention. Many of the Girondists were later executed as traitors to the Revolution.

Marat, who suffered from a chronic skin disease and other health problems, became homebound soon after the overthrow of the Girondists. He was taking a medicinal bath for his skin condition on July 13, 1793, when Charlotte Corday, a Girondist supporter, came into his apartment. She pretended to bring him information about other traitors, but when she got close to the bathtub, she stabbed Marat through the heart, killing him instantly.

Charlotte Corday was born in Saint-Saturnin, France, on July 27, 1768. She attended school in a Catholic convent and did well at her studies. In addition to completing her schoolwork, she read a great deal on her own. She especially enjoyed essays by Rousseau, Voltaire, and other thinkers of the Enlightenment who suggested that government should reflect the will of the people.

When the French Revolution began in 1789, Corday considered herself a moderate. Like many French citizens, she believed that people should have more freedom, and that the monarchy and aristocrats controlled too much of the nation's wealth and power. However, she did not feel that Louis XVI should be dethroned. Instead, she felt that a compromise could be worked out between the Third Estate and the king.

Opposite: As a Girondist, Charlotte Corday detested extremists like Marat. Above: Corday leaves the scene of the crime after stabbing Marat in his bathtub.

As the Revolution went on, however, Louis was jailed as a traitor. Corday and other moderates, known as Girondists, were discouraged when the new legislative body, the National Convention, voted to execute the king in January 1793. The Girondists who had been a part of the convention gradually lost their power to extremists led by the newspaper writer Jean-Paul Marat. As Marat continued to advocate violence, Corday became convinced that the Revolution had spun out of control and was no longer a positive instrument for change.

Corday traveled to Paris in the summer of 1793. She tricked Marat, whom she blamed for the violence, into letting her visit him in his apartment. She had sent word that she knew of antirevolutionary activity west of Paris, and she promised to give him the names of the traitors. Although Marat did not usually receive visitors in his apartment, he agreed, for he was always on the lookout for enemies of the Revolution. On July 13, 1793, Corday stabbed him through the heart as he sat in his bathtub.

She was caught by police immediately, and was sentenced to death. At her trial she called Marat a monster, and said that she was glad to have stood up to the kind of revolution that he represented. She was executed, beheaded by the guillotine, on July 17, 1793, at the age of twenty-five. Ironically, the murder of Marat resulted in the opposite of what Corday intended—it made him a martyr and led to more popular support for the extremists.

Maximilien Robespierre

Leader of the Jacobins

Maximilien Robespierre was born in Arras, France, on May 6, 1758. His father and grandfather had been lawyers, and Robespierre decided when he was young that he, too, would study law. He received his law degree from the University of Paris in 1780.

He returned to Arras and began practicing law, representing disadvantaged people in cases against the more privileged. He also spent a great deal of time reading the essays of Jean-Jacques Rousseau. Robespierre was inspired by Rousseau's ideas about honor and citizenship and vowed to begin putting the good of France above all else in his life.

In 1789 Robespierre was elected as a representative of the Third Estate in the Estates-General, an assembly called by the king to deal with the financial crisis in France. He spoke out, urging equality for all citizens, and advocated the end of discrimination against Jews, Protestants, and other minorities. This won him great popularity among the common people.

Once the Revolution began and Louis XVI was removed from power, a new assembly, called the

Opposite: A Jacobin radical, Maximilien Robespierre was one of the chief figures responsible for the Reign of Terror. Above: In 1794 Robespierre is shot and arrested.

National Convention, was formed. Robespierre was elected as a representative and became head of the Jacobins, the most radical members of the convention. He also led the attack on the more moderate members of the assembly, known as the Girondists. Robespierre and other Jacobins forced the expulsion of the Girondists in the summer of 1793. With the moderates gone, the Jacobins controlled the National Convention.

Robespierre feared that the Revolution could be thwarted by traitors and enemies. He urged his fellow delegates to the convention to be on guard against anyone who disagreed with the ideals of the Revolution. Robespierre was the most important advocate for what became the bloodiest part of the Revolution. During this time, known as the Reign of Terror, more than seventeen thousand people were accused of treason and sent to the guillotine in less than a year.

Because of his extreme beliefs, Robespierre made many enemies. Although many disagreed with his ideas, few were foolish enough to say so publicly, lest they be executed, too. Several of his enemies did plot his arrest, however, and ordered his death. He, like so many before him, went to the guillotine on July 28, 1794.

NAPOLEON BONAPARTE

GENERAL WHO ENDED THE REVOLUTION

Napoleon Bonaparte was born on August 15, 1769, on the island of Corsica in the Mediterranean Sea. Both of his parents were of the noble class, and his father was a respected lawyer. He attended military school, and at age sixteen became a second lieutenant in the French army.

After the Revolution broke out in 1789, Louis XVI secretly communicated with the governments of Austria and Prussia, asking them for help in regaining his throne. While their foreign armies invaded France, young Napoleon quickly drew the attention of revolutionary leaders because of his ability to devise brilliant strategies in battle. Even though many of his troops were inexperienced, Napoleon found ways to outmaneuver the enemy. He was promoted in 1794 to brigadier general—a most unusual post for a young man of twenty-four.

Napoleon returned to Paris in 1795, and helped protect the National Convention at the royal palace. Delegates there were trying to write a constitution for the new republic, and they were being attacked by mobs who had been encouraged by antirevolutionaries. When the mobs began to storm the palace, Napoleon's artillery forces fired cannon at them, clearing the streets quickly. When the convention formed its new government, Napoleon was promoted to major general of all French forces. He spent the next four years defeating almost every nation in Europe—including Austria, Italy, and Prussia.

Though he contributed a great deal to the Revolution as a leader in the army, Napoleon is best known for a military coup, or government takeover, in 1799. By then the new government was no longer effective, and the French people were weary of the violence and chaos of the Revolution. With help from his supporters in the army, Napoleon took over the government on November 9 and 10, 1799, giving himself the title of consul.

The French people were relieved when Napoleon put an end to the violence by establishing a strong police force. He was a gifted politician, and created a government staffed by capable and talented assistants. Under Napoleon, new laws were written, with a number of codes that guaranteed personal liberty and religious freedom. The French people voted in 1804 to make him emperor for life.

After his coronation, Napoleon returned to military life, hoping to win more territory for France. He was defeated at the Battle of Waterloo in 1815, however, and gave up his throne. He died of cancer on May 5, 1821.

General Napoleon Bonaparte seized control of France in 1799 and put an end to the violence of the French Revolution.

1762	Jean-Jacques Rousseau publishes *The Social Contract,* in which he insists that governments need to be sensitive to the rights of all citizens.
June 11, 1775	Louis XVI becomes king of France.
1776	The American colonies declare their independence from England.
May 5, 1789	The Estates-General convenes at Versailles.
June 17, 1789	The Third Estate and supporters create the National Assembly.
July 14, 1789	Paris mobs take over the Bastille.

In 1799 French officials take an oath of loyalty to Napoleon after the general seized power through a coup.

In 1804 Napoleon crowns himself Emperor of France as Pope Pius VII and other dignitaries look on.

September 20, 1792	The recently created National Convention meets for the first time.
January 21, 1793	Louis XVI is executed in Paris.
July 13, 1793	Charlotte Corday assassinates Jean-Paul Marat, a leader of the Jacobins.
September 1793	The Reign of Terror begins, in which more than seventeen thousand people are executed as enemies of the Revolution.
November 9–19, 1799	Napoleon Bonaparte seizes power in France.
1804	Napoleon is crowned emperor of France.

FOR FURTHER INFORMATION

BOOKS

Gerald Hausman, *Napoleon and Josephine: The Sword and the Hummingbird.* New York: Orchard Books, 2004.

Tum McGowen, *Robespierre and the French Revolution in World History.* Berkeley Heights, NJ: Enslow, 2000.

Nancy Plain, *Louis XVI, Marie-Antoinette, and the French Revolution.* New York: Benchmark Books, 2002.

Stewart Russ, *The French Revolution.* Austin, TX: Raintree Steck-Vaugn, 2003.

WEB SITES

The French Revolution (www.fordham.edu/halsall/mod/modsbook.13.html). This very helpful site offers firsthand accounts, letters, and travelogues by people who witnessed the French Revolution.

Liberty, Equality, Fraternity: Exploring the French Revolution (www.chmm.gmu.edu/revolution/about.html). This excellent site contains political cartoons, revolutionary songs, and essays from the period. Also gives good information about causes of events and key revolutionary leaders.

ABOUT THE AUTHOR

Gail B. Stewart received her undergraduate degree from Gustavus Adolphus College in St. Peter, Minnesota. She did her graduate work in English, linguistics, and curriculum study at the College of St. Thomas and the University of Minnesota. She taught English and reading for more than ten years.

She has written over ninety books for young people, including a series for Lucent Books called The Other America. She has written many books on historical topics such as World War I and the Warsaw ghetto.

Stewart and her husband live in Minneapolis with their three sons, Ted, Elliot, and Flynn; two dogs; and a cat. When she is not writing, she enjoys reading, walking, and watching her sons play soccer.

INDEX

American Revolution, 4, 13, 14, 18

Bastille, 24
beheadings, 8, 33, 38
Bonaparte, Napoleon. *See* Napoleon I

Chamber of Deputies, 29
Committee of Public Safety, 34
common people, 4, 17, 18, 21, 24, 30, 37, 41. *See also* Third Estate
Common Sense, 13
constitutional monarchy, 7–8, 17, 27
Continental Army, 27
Corday, Charlotte, 37, 38–39
coup, military, 42

Danton, Georges, 34–35
de Launay, Bernard, 24–25
death sentence, 33
democracy, 10
discrimination, 41

Enlightenment, 4, 10, 21, 38
equality, 10, 41
essays, 13
estates, 4
Estates-General, 6, 21, 30, 34, 41
executions, 8, 14, 33, 34, 37, 38

First Estate, 4, 21, 30
Franklin, Benjamin, 13
freedom, 10, 42

George III, 13
Girondists, 8, 13, 37, 38, 41
Guillotin, Joseph-Ignace, 32–33
guillotine, 8, 33, 38, 41

Jacobins, 8, 13, 27, 30, 34, 37, 41

king, 4, 7–8

Lafayette, Gilbert du Motier de (Marquis de), 26–29
liberty, 10, 13, 42
Locke, John, 21
Louis XVI, 6, 7, 8, 10, 13, 14–15, 17, 18, 21, 24, 30, 34, 38, 41, 42

Marat, Jean-Paul, 34, 36–37, 38
Marie-Antoinette, 14–15, 16–17, 27
military coup, 42
Mirabeau, Comte. See Riqueti, Honoré–Gabriel
monarchy, 4, 10, 14, 37, 38
Monroe, James, 13

Napoleon I, 9, 29, 42–43
National Assembly, 6–7, 17, 21, 23, 24, 30, 33
National Convention, 13, 34, 37, 38, 41, 42
National Guard, 27
Necker, Jacques, 18–19
newspaper, 37, 38
noble class, 4, 27, 30, 42

orator, 34

Paine, Thomas, 12–13
People's Friend, The, 37
prison, 13, 24, 27

quartering, 33

Reign of Terror, 8, 34, 41
riots, 5–6, 14
Riqueti, Honoré–Gabriel, 30–31
Robespierre, Maximilien, 34, 40–41
Rousseau, Jean-Jacques, 4, 10–11, 21, 39, 41

Second Estate, 4, 30
September Massacre, 37
Sieyes, Emmanuel, 20–23
Social Contract, The, 4, 10
social justice, 10
social order, 4
State of the Finances of France, 18

taxes, 4, 5–6, 14, 17, 18
Tennis Court Oath, 7, 21
Third Estate, 4, 6–7, 14, 21, 30, 33, 38, 41
treason, 8, 13, 14, 17, 34, 38, 41
Tribune of the People, 30

Versailles, 14
violence, 8, 34, 37, 38

Washington, George, 27
What is the Third Estate?, 21